The Bletchley Collection

by Joanne Scrace

First edition
December 2014

Copyright
Eden Cottage Yarns Ltd

Photography: Victoria Magnus
Technical editing: Rachel Atkinson
Layout: Clare Devine

Published by: Eden Cottage Yarns Ltd

Printed in the UK

Eden Cottage Yarns

**Download e-book
from Ravelry.com
with code
TBCRME8W4PC**

Contents

Tunny

Hut 8

Baudot

Colossus

Bombe

Morse Code

About the Designer

Joanne Scrace is a knit and crochet designer who focuses on stylish wearable pieces, usually with a seamless construction. She enjoys combining vintage inspiration with a fresh modern feel. Joanne loves working with beautiful yarns to design items that will last – the perfect antidote to fast fashion.

She has been designing knitting and crochet patterns for magazines and yarn companies since 2011. Her work has been widely published in magazines including The Knitter, Inside Crochet, Knit Now, Yarnwise and Simply Crochet. Passionate about introducing the market to fashionable, wearable crochet she launched thecrochetproject.com with Kat Goldin in 2012. Joanne combines her designing with teaching on the UK yarn festivals circuit. She is a technical editor, working for magazines and publishers such as Simply Crochet, Inside Crochet, Crafty Magazine and Kyle Publishing. She launched The Crochet Project in 2012 and has worked with independent designers such as Kat Goldin, Anniken Allis and Sara Lora.

Normally taking her inspiration from the natural world, Joanne first became interested in Bletchley Park and the code breakers story after a visit there in 2013. Her background in Software Engineering and her love of pattern and surface decoration come together for the first time in this collection.

Introduction

In May 2014, Victoria and I began discussing our plan to create a capsule collection for the Milburn 4ply range at Eden Cottage Yarns, a luxury blend of 85% British Bluefaced Leicester and 15% silk. Encompassing both knitting and crochet patterns, the collection showcases the versatility of this beautiful yarn. Passionate about knitting for a purpose, Victoria and I were keen that the designs had a strong emphasis on wearable, everyday wardrobe staples to take you through every season. Milburn is just too nice to knit it and pop it in a drawer for safe keeping. This lustrous and silky yarn cries out to be worn at every opportunity. With the strength and sheen of the silk, the softness of the Bluefaced Leicester and a relatively high twist, it is soft enough to wear next to the skin, yet strong enough to withstand repeated wearing and washing.

On receiving the original five shades of Milburn 4ply – two more have been developed since that could easily substitute into the patterns – I was struck by the understated vintage palette. This immediately conjured images of the early twentieth century, and I decided the collection should be influenced by this era.

A year or so earlier, I had visited Bletchley Park in Buckinghamshire. Former home of Government Code and Cypher School (GC&CS, known as GCHQ from 1946 onwards) this is where Alan Turing and his team of code breakers cracked enemy cyphers. Translating the information in these messages gave the Allies the advantage in several crucial battles, enabling them to defeat the Nazis. Exploring the museum, I found the colours, shapes and imagery enthralling, and I made notes and sketches of ideas inspired by what I had seen that day. Coming from a software engineering background, I loved the idea of including themes of early computing into my design work.

Yarn, colour and inspiration collided, and I enthusiatically described my vision for the collection to Victoria, who was excited by the concept.

Over the six pieces in the collection, I explored the early computing and encoding machines and the codes of cyphers loaded into them. I wanted to connect these ideas with the design elements of items of clothing typically worn off duty, by the WRENs who manned the machines. Drawing on these influences, the shapes and styles in the patterns are a nod to the 1940s, reworked in a modern and wearable way for current times.

Joanne Scrace

About the Collection

Tunny

A versatile and structural crocheted hat, with an interesting cog-like colour pattern, inspired by the cogs on the 'Tunny' machine.

Hut 8

Hut 8 is an elegant and understated knitted cardigan. Rather like the women who manned Hut 8, it is an essential workhorse of a garment. A true wardrobe staple that will take you from day to night and work to play.

Baudot

Inspired by the encoded, punched paper tapes that were fed into the Collosus machine, the pretty lace pattern in the feminine Baudot beanie also hides a secret code: it spells out two words in the Baudot cypher, 'knit' and 'tink'.

Colossus

A heavily cabled, knitted vest, in which, although complex looking, the twenty-row repeat is easy to follow and quickly memorised, making it a satisfying knit. The pattern reflects the level of detail that would have been needed when building the original Colossus, with the cables flowing up the straps and pretty cabled waist shaping that both echoes the main pattern and flatters the figure. It is worked seamlessly in the round to the under arms, where it is split and the back and front are worked separately in rows.

Bombe

The bright drums of the Bombe machine are stylised into knitted colour work in this warm and practical cowl. As each colour work section uses just a few grams of 4ply yarn, the project is a great stash buster. You could use it as a memory project, to use up the last scraps of precious yarns and showcase them on a neutral background. You could even hide your own yarn code in the pattern.

Morse Code

The shape of this piece is particularly reminiscent of the 1940s, with the patterned yoke separated by a band. This sleek and stylish crocheted cardigan is wearable, yet makes a statement. Blending the neutral blue of 'Night Sky', with the pop of mustard from 'Harvest Gold' on the pattern, cuffs, hems and button bands creates a cardigan that will turn heads. Worked from the top down, with set in sleeves, this garment is a sophisticated project for an intermediate crocheter.

The Designs

Tunny

The spiked cogs of the Lorenz cypher, codenamed the 'Tunny', inspired the cog-like colour pattern on this hat.

Ever since watching Carrie's War - a BBC adaptation of the book by Nina Bawden - as a young girl, I've been mildly obsessed with colourwork tams. She may not even have had one, but in my head, or maybe the book, she does, so I knew I wanted to include one in this collection. This crocheted version has the advantage of giving a Fair Isle feel to the design, without the complication of stranding the colours, as each one is worked in turn. The circular, spiked pattern would be tricky to achieve if knitted, but these crochet stitches are simple and easily memorised.

The hat is crocheted in the round, from the top down, with the pattern being worked on the sides only, to keep the increases simple. The brim is worked perpendicular to the crown and allows a finer degree of adjustment on the brim, to achieve a perfect fit.

The pattern is suitable for adventurous beginners upwards, and for the more experienced crocheter, it is a quick and satisfying project.

Materials

Eden Cottage Yarns Milburn (4ply/Fingering weight; 85% Bluefaced Leicester Wool, 15% Silk; 200m / 218yds per 50g skein)
1 skein for each size in each of the following shades:
MC: Rust
CC1: Harvest Gold
CC2: Night Sky

Hooks and Accessories

3.5mm (US E/4) crochet hook
3mm (US C/2-D/3) hook
Tapestry needle

Gauge

22 sts and 12 rows to 10cm (4in) over treble crochet using 3.5mm hook or size needed to achieve gauge, after blocking.

Sizes

S (M, L)
To fit head circumference:
51 (56, 61)cm / 20 (22, 24)in
Finished brim circumference:
48.5 (53.5, 58.5)cm / 19 (21, 23)in
Finished hat body circumference:
66 (71, 76)cm / 26 (28, 30)in

Pattern Notes

Worked from the crown down in the round with RS facing. The brim is worked back and forth in rows that are attached to the body of the hat with slip stitches.

Turning chains do not count as a stitch.

Special Stitches

3trcl (three treble cluster): [Yrh, insert hook in next st, yrh, draw up a loop, yrh, pull through 2 loops] three times, yrh draw through 4 loops on the hook.

4trcl (four treble cluster): [Yrh, insert hook in next st, yrh, draw up a loop, yrh, pull through 2 loops] four times, yrh draw through 5 loops on the hook.

7trcl (seven treble cluster): [Yrh, insert hook in next st, yrh, draw up a loop, yrh, pull through 2 loops] seven times, yrh draw through 8 loops on the hook.

Shell: Work 7tr in next st.

Pattern

Crown

Rnd 1: With MC and larger hook, working into a magic ring, 3ch, 16tr, sl st to join. 16 sts

Rnd 2: 3ch, 2tr in each tr around, sl st to join. 32 sts

Rnd 3: 3ch, *1tr, 2tr in next st; rep from * around, sl st to join. 48 sts

Rnd 4: 3ch, *2tr, 2tr in next st; rep from * around, sl st to join. 64 sts

Rnd 5: 3ch, *3tr, 2tr in next st; rep from * around, sl st to join. 80 sts

Rnd 6: 3ch, *4tr, 2tr in next st; rep from * around, sl st to join. 96 sts

Rnd 7: 3ch, *5tr, 2tr in next st; rep from * around, sl st to join. 112 sts

Rnd 8: 3ch, 112tr, sl st to join.

Rnd 9: 3ch, *6tr, 2tr in next st; rep from * around, sl st to join. 128 sts

Rnd 10: 3ch, 128tr, sl st to join.

Rnd 11: 3ch, *7tr, 2tr in next st; rep from * around, sl st to join. 144 sts

Sizes M and L ONLY:

Rnd 12: 3ch, 144tr, sl st to join.

Rnd 13: 3ch, *8tr, 2tr in next st; rep from * around, sl st to join. 160 sts

Size L ONLY:

Rnd 14: 3ch, 160tr, sl st to join.

Rnd 15: 3ch, *9tr, 2tr in next st; rep from * around, sl st to join. 176 sts

Pattern section

ALL sizes again:

Rnd 1: Continuing in MC, 1ch, *1dc, miss 3 sts, shell in next st, miss 3 sts; rep from * around, sl st to join. 18 (20, 22) shells

Rnd 2: Join in CC1, 3ch, 4trcl, 3ch, *1dc, 3ch, 7trcl, 3ch; rep from * to last 4 sts, 1dc, 3ch, 3trcl, sl st to join.

Rnd 3: Continuing in CC1, 3ch, 4tr in top of 3trcl, *1dc in dc, shell in 7trcl; rep from * to last dc, 1dc in dc, 3tr in 3trcl, sl st to join.

Rnd 4: Join in CC2, 1ch, *1dc, 3ch, 7trcl, 3ch; rep from * around, sl st to join.

Rnd 5: Continuing in CC2, 1ch, *1dc in dc, shell in 7trcl; rep from * around, sl st to join. Break CC2.

Rnd 6: With CC1, 3ch, 4trcl, 3ch, *1dc, 3ch, 7trcl, 3ch; rep from * to last 4 sts, 1dc, 3ch, 3trcl, sl st to join.

Rnd 7: Continuing in CC1, 3ch, 4tr in top of 3trcl, *1dc in dc, shell in 7trcl; rep from * to last dc, 1dc in dc, 3tr in 3trcl, sl st to join. Break CC1.

Rnd 8: With MC, 1ch, *1dc, 3ch, 7trcl, 3ch; rep from * around, sl st to join.

Decreasing for brim

Rnd 1: Continuing in MC to end, 3ch, *1tr in dc, 2tr in 3ch-sp, 1tr in top of 7trcl, 2tr in 3ch-sp; rep from * around, sl st to join. 108 (120, 132) sts

Rnd 2: 3ch, *tr2tog, 4tr; rep from * around, sl st to join. 90 (100, 110) sts

Size L ONLY:
Rnd 3: 3ch, 110 tr, sl st to join.

Brim

ALL sizes again:
Without breaking yarn, change to smaller hook, 6ch.

Working in rows continue as follows:
Row 1 (RS): Starting in second ch from the hook, 4htr, sl st in next 2 sts on body of hat, turn.

Row 2 (WS): 4htr, turn.
Row 3: 2ch, 4htr, sl st in next 2 sts on body of hat, turn.

Rep rows 2 and 3 until all sts have been used. Sl st row ends together to close the brim.

Finishing

Weave in ends and block lightly.

Hut 8

Hut 8 is my homage to the civilian staff who carried out routine administrative tasks, such as punching holes in cards and filing messages, which was crucial to supporting the efforts of the code breakers. Around 130 women worked on these admin tasks and are arguably the unsung heroes of the war.

Hut 8 is an elegant and understated knitted cardigan. Rather like the women who manned Hut 8, it is an essential workhorse of a garment. A true wardrobe staple that will take you from day to night and work to play.

I became a little obsessed with codes whilst working on the collection, and you will notice that the number 8 is repeated throughout the pattern. How many eights can you find, code breaker?

The cardigan is knitted seamlessly, in one piece, from the top down, which allows for easy adjustment for fit. The three quarter length sleeves are worked in the round from live stitches, with the button band being worked as you go, meaning there is minimal finishing required.

....- - / ---..

Materials

Eden Cottage Yarns Milburn (4ply/Fingering weight; 85% Bluefaced Leicester Wool, 15% Silk; 200m / 218yds per 50g skein)
Shade: Steel x 5 (5, 6, 6, 7, 8, 8, 9, 10) skeins

Needles and Accessories

3.25mm (US 3) circular needle, minimum 80cm / 32in length
3.25mm (US 3) needles suitable for working small circumferences in the round for sleeves
4 stitch markers
2 stitch holders or waste yarn
Tapestry Needle
12 (13, 13, 13, 14, 14, 14, 15, 15) buttons, 1.5cm / 0.5in diameter
Matching thread and sewing needle

Gauge

24 sts and 36 rows to 10 cm (4in) over stocking stitch using 3.25mm needles or size needed to achieve gauge. Ensure your gauge worked in the round for the sleeves matches your gauge when working flat.

Pattern Notes

Hut 8 is worked in rows from the top down, seamlessly in one piece. Sleeve stitches are put on hold and worked afterwards in the round.
Buttonholes are worked over two rows decreasing one stitch on the first row and replacing it on the second row.

Sizes

XS (S, M, L, 1X, 2X, 3X, 4X, 5X)

Finished bust: 77 (82.5, 95.5, 104, 114, 125.5, 134, 146, 155)cm / 30.25 (32.5, 37.5, 41, 45, 49.5, 57.5, 61)in designed to be worn with 2.5cm / 1in ease at bust

Finished length: 52.5 (53, 57, 57, 57, 61.5, 61.5, 61.5, 66)cm / 20.75 (20.75, 22.5, 22.5, 22.5, 24.25, 24.25, 24.25, 26)in

Sleeve length to underarm: 26cm / 10.25in

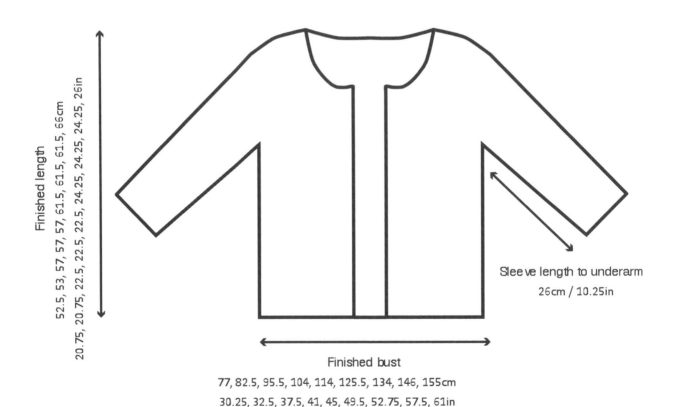

Finished length
52.5, 53, 57, 57, 57, 61.5, 61.5, 61.5, 66cm
20.75, 20.75, 22.5, 22.5, 22.5, 24.25, 24.25, 24.25, 26in

Sleeve length to underarm
26cm / 10.25in

Finished bust
77, 82.5, 95.5, 104, 114, 125.5, 134, 146, 155cm
30.25, 32.5, 37.5, 41, 45, 49.5, 52.75, 57.5, 61in

Pattern

Using longer circular needle, cast on 140 (140, 152, 152, 152, 164, 164, 176, 176) sts.

Rolled Collar

Row 1 (RS): Knit.
Row 2 (WS): Purl.
Rows 3 and 4: Knit.

Commence yoke increases as follows:

Row 1 (RS)(Inc): K16 (16, 13, 13, 21, 16, 19, 13, 13), *kfb, k5 (5, 6, 5, 4, 5, 4, 5, 5); rep from * to last 10 (10, 6, 7, 16, 10, 15, 7, 7) sts, k to end. 19 (19, 19, 22, 23, 23, 26, 26, 26) sts inc; 159 (159, 171, 174, 175, 187, 190, 202, 202) sts

Row 2 (WS): Knit.

Row 3 (Buttonhole): K to last 6 sts, k2tog, yo, k2togtbl, k2. 158 (158, 170, 173, 174, 186, 189, 201, 201) sts
Row 4 (Buttonhole): K3, kfb into yo from last row, k to end. 159 (159, 171, 174, 175, 187, 190, 202, 202) sts

Rows 5-6: Knit.
Row 7 (Inc): K16 (16, 13, 13, 21, 16, 19, 13, 13), *kfb, k6 (6, 7, 6, 5, 6, 5, 6, 6); rep from * to last 10 (10, 6, 7, 16, 10, 15, 7, 7) sts, k to end. 19 (19, 19, 22, 23, 23, 26, 26, 26) sts inc; 178 (178, 190, 196, 198, 210, 216, 228, 228) sts

Row 8: Knit.

Row 9: Knit.
Row 10: K8, p to last 8 sts, k8.

Rows 11-16: Rep last 2 rows a further 3 times.
Last 16 rows set patt.

Work these 16 rows a total of 4 (5, 5, 5, 6, 6, 6, 7, 7) times to 292 (330, 342, 372, 428, 440, 476, 540, 540) sts

Note: Work 1 extra stitch in the increase repeat on every subsequent increase row as follows:

Next (third) inc row: K16 (16, 13, 13, 21, 16, 19, 13, 13), *kfb, k7 (7, 8, 7, 6, 7, 6, 7, 7); rep from * to last 10 (10, 6, 7, 16, 10, 15, 7, 7) sts, k to end.

Next (fourth) inc row: K16 (16, 13, 13, 21, 16, 19, 13, 13), *kfb, k8 (8, 9, 8, 7, 8, 7, 8, 8); rep from * to last 10 (10, 6, 7, 16, 10, 15, 7, 7) sts, k to end.

Continue working 1 more st in each subsequent increase as set.

Sizes XS, M, L, 2X, 3X and 5X ONLY:

Work the 16-row repeat once more replacing Row 7 with a knit row (ie. do not increase). 311 (-, 361, 394, -, 463, 502, -, 566) sts

ALL sizes again:

Split the yoke into body and sleeves:
Next Row (RS): K47 (50, 57, 63, 68, 72, 78, 84, 88), slip next 65 (68, 70, 76, 83, 91, 100, 107, 111) sts to holder, using knitted-on method, cast on 6 (6, 8, 8, 10, 14, 14, 16, 18) sts, k87 (94, 107, 116, 126, 137, 146, 158, 168) sts, slip next 65 (68, 70, 76, 83, 91, 100, 107, 111) sts to holder, using knitted-on method, cast on 6 (6, 8, 8, 10, 14, 14, 16, 18) sts, k47 (50, 57, 63, 68, 72, 78, 84, 88) sts. 193 (206, 237, 258, 282, 309, 330, 358, 380) sts remain for Body

Body

Next Row (WS): K8, p to last 8 sts, k8.
Next Row (RS) (Buttonhole): K2, k2tog, yo, k2togtbl, k to end.

Next Row (Buttonhole): K3, kfb into yo from last row, k3, p to last 8 sts, k8.

Work straight in St st with garter st button bands, as set for 35 (35, 27, 27, 27, 27, 19, 39, 39) rows, placing buttonholes every 16th row and ending with a RS row.

Waist Shaping

Next Row (WS): K8, p17 (19, 23, 26, 29, 32, 35, 38, 41), pm, p56 (60, 69, 75, 82, 90, 96, 104, 110), pm, p31 (32, 37, 40, 44, 49, 52, 58, 62), pm, p56 (60, 69, 75, 82, 90, 96, 104, 110), pm, p17 (19, 23, 26, 29, 32, 35, 38, 41), k8. 4 markers placed for waist shaping

Next Row (RS)(Dec row): [K to marker, sm, ssk, k to 2 sts before marker, k2tog, sm] twice, k to end. 4 sts dec

Work 7 (7, 7, 7, 7, 7, 7, 3, 3) rows straight in St st with garter st button bands continuing to place buttonholes as set.

Rep last 8 (8, 8, 8, 8, 8, 8, 4, 4) rows a further 4 (4, 5, 5, 5, 5, 6, 8, 8) times then work dec row again once more. 169 (182, 209, 230, 254, 281, 298, 318, 340) sts

Work straight in St st and garter st pattern as set for 8 rows.
Next Row (RS)(Inc): [K to marker, sm, kfb, k to 2 sts before marker, kfb, k1, sm] twice, k to end. 4 sts inc

Next row (WS): Work in St st and garter st pattern as set.

Rep last 2 rows a further 7 times continuing to place buttonholes as set. 201 (214, 241, 262, 286, 313, 330, 350, 372) sts

Work 2 rows in St st and garter st pattern as set.

Rolled Hem

Knit 9 rows, continuing to place buttonholes as set.
Next Row (WS): Purl.

Cast off.

Sleeves

With RS facing, using needles suitable for working small circumferences in the round, pick up and k6 (6, 8, 8, 10, 14, 14, 16, 18) sts from underarm, then slip held sts back onto needle arrange sleeve sts evenly around the needles and knit, pm at centre of underarm cast-on section for beginning of round. 71 (74, 78, 84, 93, 105, 114, 123, 129) sts
Note: Work following Sleeve decrease round as follows: K2tog, k to last 2 sts, ssk.

Work St st in the round (knit every round), dec at start and end of round every 10 (11, 11, 11, 8, 6, 5, 4, 4) rounds until stitch count is 53 (58, 60, 66, 69, 71, 78, 81, 83) sts
Work straight in St st until sleeve measure 25cm / 9.75in from underarm.

Rolled Cuff

Next rnd: Purl.
Next rnd: Knit.

Rep last 2 rounds a further 3 times.
Knit 3 rounds.

Cast off.

Finishing

Weave in ends and block lightly.

Using buttonholes as a guide for placement, sew on buttons.

.... ..- - / ---..

Baudot

When I first saw the punched paper tapes that were fed into the Collosus machine, they reminded me of lace ribbons. I was determined to create a pattern that had a secret code within it, much like the punched paper tapes that I had been unable to get out of my mind. The pretty lace pattern in the feminine Baudot beanie also hides a secret: it spells out two words in the Baudot cypher, 'knit' and 'tink'.

Tink is a colloquial term to describe the action of 'un-knitting', where a mistake is carefully rectified by undoing each stitch back to where the mistake occurred. Tink is knit spelt backwards.

Hopefully, this easy lace pattern will see you doing more knitting than tinking! The hat is worked in the round, from the brim to the crown, using just one 50g skein. The crown is lightly gathered, rather than decreased, giving a lovely, soft shape.

Materials

Eden Cottage Yarns Milburn (4ply/Fingering weight; 85% Bluefaced Leicester Wool, 15% Silk; 200m / 218yds per 50g skein)
Shade: Damson x 2 skeins

Needles and Accessories

3.25mm (US 3) circular needle, 40cm / 16in length or DPNs
3.5mm (US 4) circular needle, 40cm / 16in length or DPNs
Stitch marker
Tapestry needle

Gauge

26 sts and 28 rows to 10cm (4in) over lace pattern using 3.5mm needles or size needed to achieve gauge, after blocking.

Sizes

S (M, L)
To fit head circumference:
51 (56, 61)cm / 20 (22, 24)in
Finished brim circumference:
48.5 (53.5, 58.5)cm / 19 (21, 23)in

Pattern Notes

Baudot is worked from the brim up in a lace pattern before softly gathering at the top.
Lace pattern instructions are both charted and written in full.

Pattern

Using smaller needles, cast on 132 (144, 156). Taking care not to twist the sts, join to work in the round, and place marker for beginning of round.

Brim

Rnd 1: *K1, p1; rep from * to end.
Rnd 2: Knit.
Rep last 2 rounds a further 7 times.
Next Rnd: *K11, kfb; rep from * around. 143 (156, 169) sts

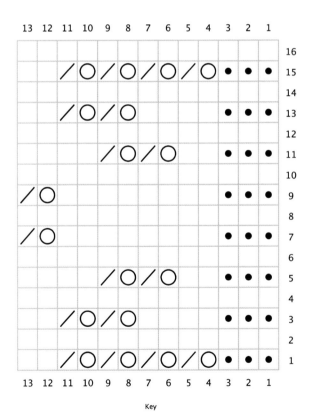

Key

knit   ● purl   ○ yo   / k2tog

Main Hat

Using larger needles, working from chart or written instructions below, commence lace pattern working the 13-st repeat 11 (12, 13) times across the round:

Rnd 1: *P3, [yo, k2tog] 4 times, k2; rep from * around.

Rnd 2 and all even numbered rounds: Knit.

Rnd 3: *P3, k4, [yo, k2tog] twice, k2; rep from * to end.

Rnd 5: *P3, k2, [yo, k2tog] twice, k4; rep from * to end.

Rnds 7 and 9: *P3, k8, yo, k2tog; rep from * to end.

Rnd 11: *P3, k2, [yo, k2tog] twice, k4; rep from * to end.

Rnd 13: *P3, k4, [yo, k2tog] twice, k2; rep from * to end.

Rnd 15: *P3, [yo, k2tog] 4 times, k2; rep from * around.

Rounds 1-16 set lace pattern.

Rep lace pattern a further 3 (3, 4) times.

Note: If you would like a slouchier hat, work more repeats of lace pattern ending with round 8 or 16 to keep the code intact.

Break yarn leaving a 20cm / 8in tail.

Finishing

Thread tail onto tapestry needle, pass through all stitches on the needles twice, pulling tight to close the hole and fasten yarn securely.

Weave in loose ends and block lightly.

Colossus

Designed to assist the code breakers with their work, Colossus was the first programmable digital computer. Technology that would probably now fit on your fingertip took up a whole room with each connection being a physical cable, rather than tiny slivers of silicon. There are cables everywhere, weaving in and out across the machine, all carrying vital information. This complex mess, that was helping to make sense of hidden messages, became the inspiration for this heavily cabled knitted vest.

The cables are a little more orderly in the knitted version of Colossus, the twenty-row repeat is easy to follow and quickly memorised, making it a satisfying knit. The pattern reflects the level of detail that would have been needed when building the original Colossus, with the cables flowing up the straps and pretty cabled waist shaping that both echoes the main pattern and flatters the figure. It is worked seamlessly in the round to the under arms, where it is split and the back and front are worked separately in rows.

With all the sophistication of 1940s fashion, this elegant and modern piece looks equally good layered over a shirt for the office as it does with a long sleeved tee and jeans at leisure.

Materials

Eden Cottage Yarns Milburn (4ply/Fingering weight; 85% Bluefaced Leicester Wool, 15% Silk; 200m / 218yds per 50g skein)
Shade: Damson x 3 (4, 4, 4, 5, 5, 5, 5, 6) skeins

Needles and Accessories

3.5mm (US 4) circular needle 60 (60, 60, 80, 80, 80, 100, 100, 100)cm / 24 (24, 24, 32, 32, 32, 40, 40, 40)in length
3.25mm (US 3) circular needle, 40cm / 16in length

Cable needle
4 removable stitch markers
2 stitch holders or waste yarn

Gauge

28 sts and 32 rows to 10cm (4in) over 4x4 rib using 3.5mm needles or size needed to achieve gauge.

Sizes

XS (S, M, L, 1X, 2X, 3X, 4X, 5X)

Finished bust: 87 (93, 98, 110, 122, 133, 139, 145, 157)cm / 34.25 (36.5, 38.75, 43.5, 48, 52.5, 54.75, 57.25, 61.75)in

Finished length: 57 (58, 60, 61, 62, 63, 65, 66, 67) cm / 22.5 (23, 23.5, 24, 24.5, 25, 25.5, 26, 26.5)in

Armhole depth: 19 (20, 22, 23, 24, 25, 27, 28, 29)cm / 7.5 (8, 8.5, 9, 9.5, 10, 10.5, 11, 11.5)in

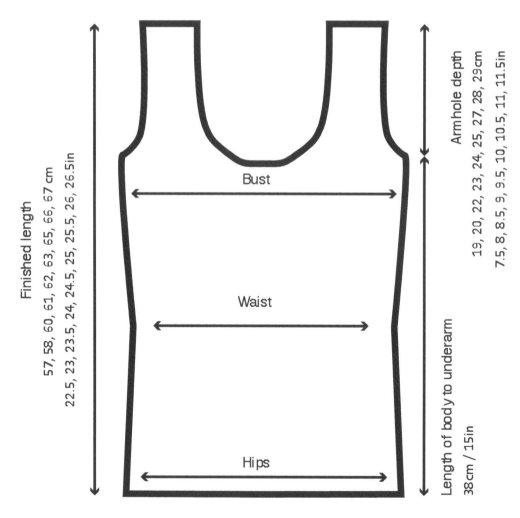

Finished length
57, 58, 60, 61, 62, 63, 65, 66, 67 cm
22.5, 23, 23.5, 24, 24.5, 25, 25.5, 26, 26.5in

Armhole depth
19, 20, 22, 23, 24, 25, 27, 28, 29cm
7.5, 8, 8.5, 9, 9.5, 10, 10.5, 11, 11.5in

Length of body to underarm
38cm / 15in

Bust

Waist

Hips

Bust and hips
87 (93, 98, 110, 122, 133, 139, 145, 157)cm /
34.25 (35.5, 38.75, 43.5, 48, 52.5, 54.75, 57.25, 61.75)in

Waist
76 (81, 87, 98, 110, 122, 128, 133, 145)cm /
29.75 (32, 34.25, 38.75, 43.5, 48, 50.25, 52.5, 57.25)in

Special Stitches

Cables

C4B: Sl 2 sts to cn and hold at back, k2 from LH needle, k2 from cn.

C4F: Sl 2 sts to cn and hold at front, k2 from LH needle, k2 from cn.

T4B: Sl 2 sts to cn and hold at back, k2 from LH needle, p2 from cn.

T4F: Sl 2 sts to cn and hold at front, p2 from LH needle, k2 from cn.

Increases

RLI (right leaning increase): Insert LH needle from back to front under thread running between two stitches, knit it.

LLI (left leaning increase): Insert LH needle from front to back under thread running between two stitches, knit it through the back loop.

RLIP (right leaning increase, purled): Insert LH needle from back to front under thread running between two stitches, purl it.

LLIP (left leaning increase, purled): Insert LH needle from front to back under thread running between two stitches, purl it through the back loop.

Stitch Patterns

1x1 Rib

Every Rnd: *K1, p1; rep from * to end.

4x4 Rib

Every Rnd: *K4, p4; rep from * to end.

Cable Pattern

When worked in the round:

Rnd 1: P4, *C4B, p4; rep from * to marker.

Rnds 2-4: P4, *k4, p4; rep from * to marker.

Rnds 5-12: Rep Rnds 1-4 twice more.

Rnd 13: P4, *C4B, p4; rep from * to marker.

Rnd 14: P4, *k4, p4; rep from * to marker.

Rnd 15: P2, *T4B, T4F; rep from * to 2 sts before marker, p2.

Rnd 16: P2, *k2, p4, k2; rep from * to 2 sts before marker, p2.

Rnd 17: P2, k2, *p4, C4F; rep from * to 8 sts before marker, p4, k2, p2.

Rnd 18: P2, *k2, p4, k2; rep from * to 2 sts before marker, p2.

Rnd 19: P2, *T4F, T4B; rep from * to 2 sts before marker, p2.

Rnd 20: P4, *k4, p4; rep from * to marker.

Repeat Rounds 1-20 for pattern.

Cable Pattern

When worked back and forth in rows:

Row 1 (RS): P4, *C4B, p4; rep from * to marker.

Row 2 (WS): K4, *p4, k4; rep from * to marker.

Row 3: P4, *k4, p4; rep from * to marker.

Row 4: K4, *p4, k4; rep from * to marker.

Rows 5-12: Rep rows 1-4.

Row 13: P4, *C4B, p4; rep from * to marker.

Row 14: K4, *p4, k4; rep from * to marker.

Row 15: P2, *T4B, T4F; rep from * to 2 sts before marker, p2.

Row 16: K2, *p2, k4, p2; rep from * to 2 sts before marker, k2.

Row 17: P2, k2, *p4, C4F; rep from * to 8 sts before marker, p4, k2, p2.

Row 18: K2, *p2, k4, p2; rep from * to 2 sts before marker, k2.

Row 19: P2, *T4F, T4B; rep from * to 2 sts before marker, p2.

Row 20: K4, *p4, k4; rep from * to marker.

Repeat Rows 1-20 for pattern.

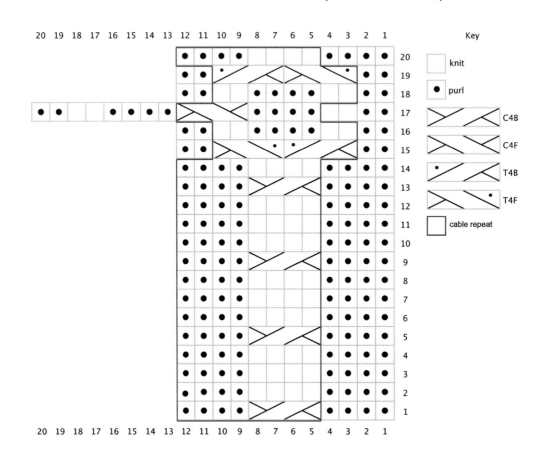

Key

☐ knit

● purl

C4B

C4F

T4B

T4F

☐ cable repeat

Pattern

Using larger needles, cast on 240 (256, 272, 304, 336, 368, 384, 400, 432) sts. Being careful not to twist, join to work in the round, and pm for start of round.

Work 4x4 rib until fabric measures 5cm / 2in.

Set-up for cable pattern as follows:

Next Rnd: Working in rib as set, [rib 44 sts, pm, rib 76 (84, 92, 108, 124, 140, 148, 156, 172) sts, pm] twice. 4 markers placed (fourth marker will be existing start of round marker)

Working cable pattern in the round from the chart or written instructions, continue as follows:

Rnds 1-12: [rib to marker, work cable pattern to next marker] twice.

Waist shaping

Rnd 1: [K4, p4, (k1, ssk, k1, p4, k1, k2tog, k1, p4) twice, k4, sm, work round 13 of cable patt, sm] twice. 232 (248, 264, 296, 328, 360, 376, 392, 424) sts

Rnd 2: [K4, p4, (k3, p4) four times, k4, sm, work next round of cable patt, sm] twice.

Rnd 3: [K4, p4, (k1, ssk, p4, k2tog, k1, p4) twice, k4, sm, work next round of cable patt, sm] twice. 224 (240, 256, 288, 320, 352, 368, 384, 416) sts

Rnd 4: [K4, p4, (k2, p4) four times, k4, sm, work next round of cable patt, sm] twice.

Rnd 5: [K4, p4, (k1, ssk, p2, k2tog, k1, p4) twice, k4, sm, work next round of cable patt, sm] twice. 216 (232, 248, 280, 312, 344, 360, 376, 408) sts

Rnd 6: [K4, p4, (k2, p2, k2, p4) twice, k4, sm, work next round of cable patt, sm] twice.

Rnd 7: [K4, p4, (k1, ssk, k2tog, k1, p4) twice, k4, sm, work next round of cable patt, sm] twice. 208 (224, 240, 272, 304, 336, 352, 368, 400) sts

Rnd 8: [K4, (p4, k4) three times, sm, work next round of cable patt (rnd 20), sm] twice.

Rnd 9: [K4, p4, (C4B, p4) twice, k4, sm, work next round of cable patt (rnd 1), sm] twice.

Rnds 10-12: Work 4x4 rib.

Rnds 13-22: Work Rnds 9-12 twice more then Rounds 9 and 10 only once more.

Rnd 23: [K4, p4, (k2, RLIP, LLIP, k2, p4) twice, k4, sm, work cable patt (rnd 15), sm] twice. 216 (232, 248, 280, 312, 344, 360, 376, 408) sts

Rnd 24: [K4, p4, (k2, p2, k2, p4) twice, k4, sm, work next round of cable patt, sm] twice.

Rnd 25: [K4, p4, (k2, RLIP, p2, LLIP, k2, p4) twice, k4, sm, work cable patt, sm] twice. 224 (240, 256, 288, 320, 352, 368, 384, 416) sts

Rnd 26: [K4, p4, (k2, p4) four times, k4, sm, work next round of cable patt, sm] twice.

Rnd 27: [K4, p4, (k2, RLI, p4, LLI, k2, p4) twice, k4, sm, work cable patt, sm] twice. 232 (248, 264, 296, 328, 360, 376, 392, 424) sts

Rnd 28: [K4, p4, (k3, p4) four times, k4, sm, work next round of cable patt, sm] twice.

Rnd 29: [K4, p4, (k3, RLI, p4, LLI, k3, p4) twice, k4, sm, work cable patt, sm] twice. 240 (256, 272, 304, 336, 368, 384, 400, 432) sts

Work straight to underarm for a further 52 rounds as follows: [Work 4x4 rib to first marker, work cable pattern to next marker] twice. You will end on Round 13 of the cable pattern.

Split for underarms and back as follows:

Work 12 (12, 12, 4, 4, 0, 0, 0, 0) sts in patt (part of Back), cast off next 20 (20, 20, 36, 36, 44, 44, 44, 44) sts (Left Underarm), work 36 (36, 36, 44, 52, 52, 60, 60, 68) sts in patt (Left Front Strap), cast off next 28 (36, 44, 28, 28, 36, 28, 36, 36) sts (Front Neckline), work 36 (36, 36, 44, 52, 52, 60, 60, 68) sts in patt (Right Front Strap), cast off 20 (20, 20, 36, 36, 44, 44, 44, 44) sts (Left Underarm), work in patt to end of rnd (remainder of Back). Break yarn. 172 (180, 188, 204, 236, 244, 268, 276, 308) sts in total – 72 (72, 72, 88, 104, 104, 120, 120, 136) sts for Front, 100 (108, 116, 116, 132, 140, 148, 156, 172) sts for Back

Place all Strap sts on holders.

Notes for continuing to work in pattern:

You will now work in rows using the Row instructions for the cable pattern. Knit the first and last stitch of each row to give a neat selvedge to pick up stitches from.

As you decrease across the pattern stitches do not work the cable unless there are at least 2 sts between the cable and the edge. Where there are not enough stitches to cable work even in pattern, ie. knit a knit stitch, purl a purl stitch.

Back

Note: When decreasing for the straps work as follows: Work one st, work left leaning dec in patt, patt to last 3 sts, work right leaning dec in patt, work last st.

Place the 100 (108, 116, 116, 132, 140, 148, 156, 172) Back sts onto larger circular needle.

With RS facing, rejoin yarn and continue in 4x4 rib and cable pattern as set starting with row 15, work cable pattern in rows as established using the full 20-row repeat and AT THE SAME TIME, dec one st at each edge on first and every following row for 6 (6, 6, 6, 10, 10, 14, 14, 18) rows then every RS row 6 (6, 6, 6, 10, 14, 14, 18) times. 76 (84, 92, 92, 92, 100, 92, 100, 100) sts

Work straight in patt until Back measures 19 (20, 22, 23, 24, 25, 27, 28, 29)cm / 7.5 (7.75, 8.75, 9, 9.5, 9.75, 10.75, 11, 11.5)in from underarm.

Cast off.

Straps (both alike)

Place Strap sts on larger circular needle.

With RS facing rejoin yarn and work in established patterns starting with cable pattern Row 3 but repeating Rows 1-4 only and AT THE SAME TIME dec one st at neck edge on first and every following row 6 times then every RS rows 6 times and AT THE SAME TIME dec one st on armhole edge on first and every row for 6 (6, 6, 6, 10, 10, 14, 14, 18) rows then every RS row 6 (6, 6, 6, 10, 10, 14, 14, 18) times. 12 (12, 12, 12, 12, 12, 20, 20, 20) sts

Work straight in patt as set until Strap measures 19 (20, 22, 23, 24, 25, 27, 28, 29)cm / 7.5 (7.75, 8.75, 9, 9.5, 9.75, 10.75, 11, 11.5)in from underarm.

Cast off. Repeat for second Strap.

Finishing

Sew shoulder seams.

Armhole Bands

Using smaller circular needle, pick up stitches evenly (approximately one st per st and 2 sts for every 3 rows) around neck edge and work in 1x1 rib for 5 rows.

Cast off in pattern.

Repeat for second armhole.

Weave in ends and block lightly.

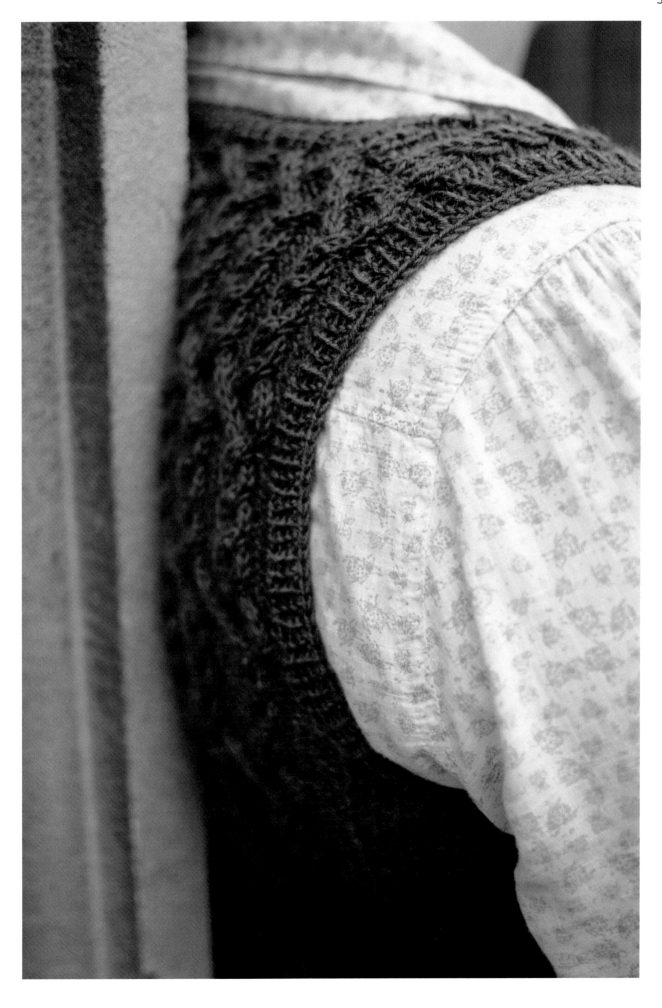

Bombe

The Bombe machine was an electromechanical device, designed by Alan Turing, to find out the daily settings on the Enigma code machine. This huge machine is made up of row upon row of brightly coloured drums, each of which emulated one of the rotors on the Enigma machine.

The bright drums of the Bombe machine are stylised into knitted colour work in this warm and practical cowl. As each colour work section uses just a few grams of 4ply yarn, the project is a great stash buster. You could use it as a memory project, to use up the last scraps of precious yarns and showcase them on a neutral background. You could even hide your own yarn code in the pattern.

Worked in the round from a provisional cast on, the cowl is grafted together, to form a seamless tube that is omnidirectional and reversible. With an easy to follow, simple, repeating pattern and zero shaping, this is an ideal first colour work project, whilst leaving lots of customisable options open for the more experienced knitter. The huge bonus to this pattern, is that all the ends are contained within the cowl, so no need for weaving in all the ends as you would with other colour work.

Materials

Eden Cottage Yarns Milburn (4ply/Fingering weight; 85% Bluefaced Leicester Wool, 15% Silk; 200m / 218yds per 50g skein)
MC: Steel x 2 skeins
CC: Small amounts of contrasting colours. Sample uses 18 x 3g (54g in total) of Damson, Harvest Gold, Night Sky and Rust

Needles and Accessories

3.25mm (US 3) circular needle, 40cm / 16in length or DPNs
1 stitch marker
Waste yarn in a similar weight for provisional cast on
Crochet hook in a similar size to needle for provisional cast on
Tapestry needle

Size

One size: 20cm / 8in width x 56cm / 22.5in length

Gauge

28 sts and 32 rows to 10cm (4in) over stocking stitch using 3.25mm needles or size needed to achieve gauge, after blocking.
Gauge is not critical but will affect finished size and yarn amounts.

Special Techniques

Grafting

Place the stitches from the provisional cast on onto a spare needle. Leave the stitches from the cast off end on the needle, position so both needles are facing right and ensure the cowl is not twisted.

The needle closest to you (with the cast-off end) is Needle A, the needle furthest (with cast-on edge) is Needle B – mark them if necessary.

Thread a length of MC yarn onto a tapestry needle.

Preliminary step: Pass tapestry needle through first stitch on Needle A as if to purl, pass through first st on Needle B as if to knit. Leave both stitches on the knitting needles.

Step 1: Pass tapestry needle through first stitch on Needle A as if to knit, drop stitch from knitting needle and draw yarn through.

Step 2: Pass tapestry needle through next stitch on Needle A as if to purl, leave it on the knitting needle.

Step 3: Pass tapestry needle through first stitch on Needle B as if to purl, drop stitch from knitting needle and draw yarn through.

Step 4: Pass tapestry needle through next stitch on Needle B as if to knit, leave stitch on knitting needle.

Repeat steps 1-4 until all but 2 stitches have been worked and dropped from knitting needles.

Work steps 1 and 3 only to graft last 2 stitches.

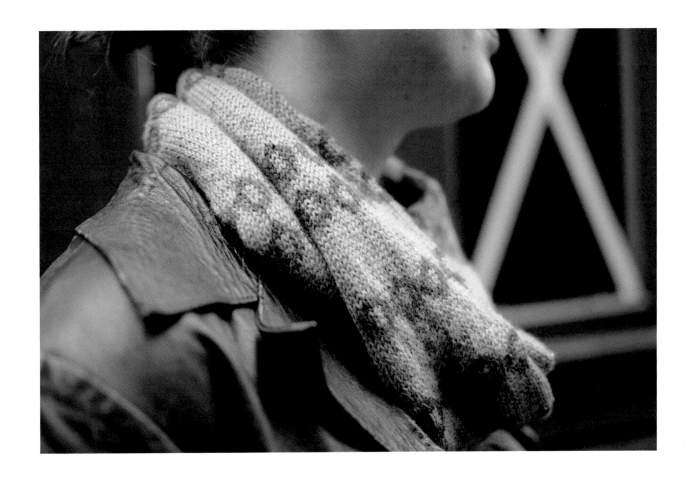

Pattern Notes

Bombe is worked in the round from a provisional cast-on allowing the ends to be grafted together for a neat finish. If preferred a standard cast on and cast off can be used and the ends sewn together with mattress stitch.

Alter the width of the cowl by casting on in multiples of 7 stitches.

Adjust the length by working more repeats of the 36-round pattern.

The number of stitches worked in either MC or CC for the colourwork pattern are given after the abbreviation, so 'MC2, CC4' translates as 'knit 2 stitches in MC, knit 4 stitches in CC'.

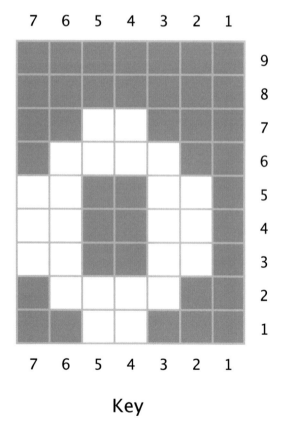

Key

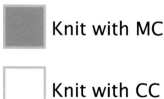

Knit with MC

Knit with CC

Pattern

Using waste yarn and the provisional crochet cast-on method, cast on 112 sts as follows:

Using the crochet hook and waste yarn, make approximately 130 chain.

Change to the knitting needle and starting in the eighth chain, thread the needle through each of the back bumps of the chain so you have 112 sts on the needle, leaving the remaining chain to prevent the stitches unravelling.

Set-up rnd: With MC, knit across all 112 sts.

Join to work in the round, being careful not to twist stitches and place marker for beginning of round.

**Knit 5 rounds.

Working from the written instructions below or chart, continue as follows:

Rnd 1: *MC3, CC2, MC2; rep from * to end.
Rnd 2: *MC2, CC4, MC1; rep from * to end.
Rnds 3-5: *MC1, CC2, MC2, CC2; rep from * to end.
Rnd 6: *MC2, CC4, MC1; rep from * to end.
Rnd 7: *MC3, CC2, MC2; rep from * to end.
Rnds 8 and 9: With MC only, knit to end.

Last 9 rounds set colourwork pattern.

Rep colourwork pattern twice more, changing CC each repeat as desired.

Knit 4 rounds in MC.**

Rep from ** to ** a further 4 times, changing CC as desired and omitting final 2 rounds on last repeat.

Finishing

Remove provisional cast on and graft the ends together.

Weave in loose ends and block lightly.

Morse Code

You simply can't have a code breaking collection without a reference to that most famous of them all: Morse Code. A simple code of dots and dashes, with the ability to convey the world's most complicated ideas and thoughts.

This cardigan took lots of development to get the colour pattern just right, much the same as the ground breaking machinery, such as Collosus and Bombe did. Inspired by the pioneering methods that Alan Turing used, I decided to use an innovative technique for the colour play that represents the code. This involves working a row twice, once in each colour, and working with the chains from the first pass held either to the back or to the front to make the dashes.

The shape of this piece is particularly reminiscent of the 1940s, with the patterned yoke separated by a band. This sleek and stylish crocheted cardigan is wearable yet makes a statement. Blending the neutral blue of 'Night Sky', with the pop of mustard from 'Harvest Gold' on the pattern, cuffs, hems and button bands creates a cardigan that will turn heads. Worked from the top down, with set in sleeves, this garment is a sophisticated make for an intermediate crocheter.

Materials

Eden Cottage Yarns Milburn (4ply/Fingering weight; 85% Bluefaced Leicester Wool, 15% Silk; 200m / 218yds per 50g skein)

MC: Night Sky x 5 (6, 6, 7, 7, 8, 8, 9, 9) skeins
CC: Harvest Gold x 1 (1, 1, 1, 1, 2, 2, 2, 2) skeins

Hooks and Accessories

3.5mm (US E/4) crochet hook
4mm (US G/6) crochet hook
4 locking stitch markers
Tapestry needle
6 buttons, 2.5cm / 1in diameter

Gauge

18 sts and 16 rows to 10 cm (4in) over half treble crochet using 4mm hook or size needed to achieve gauge, after blocking.

Pattern Notes

Back worked from neck to armholes, fronts are worked directly onto the back to the armhole and joined before working the body in one piece to the hem. Sleeves are seamlessly set in using short rows. Button bands, hems, cuffs and neckband are worked in rows attached to the cardigan as you go. Turning chains do not count as a stitch.

Sizes

XS (S, M, L, 1X, 2X, 3X, 4X, 5X)

Finished bust: 81 (90.5, 98, 111, 120, 129.5, 136, 149.5, 161.5)cm / 32 (35.75, 38.5, 43.75, 47.25, 51, 53.5, 58.75, 63.75)in

Finished length: 54.5 (56, 57, 58.5, 59.5, 61, 62, 63.5, 64.5)cm / 21.5 (22, 22.5, 23, 23.5, 24, 24.5, 25, 25.5)in

Sleeve length to underarm: 47.5cm / 18in

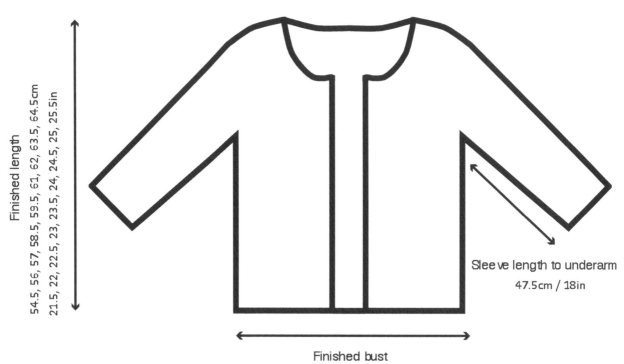

Finished length
54.5, 56, 57, 58.5, 59.5, 61, 62, 63.5, 64.5cm
21.5, 22, 22.5, 23, 23.5, 24, 24.5, 25, 25.5in

Sleeve length to underarm
47.5cm / 18in

Finished bust
81, 90.5, 98, 111, 120, 129.5, 136, 149.5, 161.5cm
32, 35.75, 38.5, 43.75, 47.25, 51, 53.5, 58.75, 63.75in

Special Stitches

5trcl (five treble cluster): [Yrh, insert into st, yrh, pull up a loop, yrh, draw through 2 loops] five times in same st, yrh, draw through all 6 loops on hook.

Pattern

Back (beginning at shoulders):

With MC and larger hook, make 51 (58, 65, 65, 65, 72, 72, 72, 72)ch.
Set-up row: Starting in third ch from hook, 1htr in each st across. 49 (56, 63, 63, 63, 70, 70, 70, 70) sts

Commence colourwork pattern as follows:

Rows 1 and 2: 2ch, 1htr in each st across. Do not break MC.

Row 3 (WS): Miss 3 sts, join CC, 3ch, begin in same st as ch, *5trcl, 8ch, miss 6 sts; rep from * to last 4 sts, 5trcl, miss last 3 sts. Fasten off and break CC.
Without turning start again at the beginning of the row with MC, 2ch, 3htr, *1dc in top of 5trcl, 2htr with CC ch in front of hook, 2htr with CC ch behind hook, 2htr with CC ch in front of hook; rep from * to last 4 sts, 1dc in top of 5trcl, 3htr.

Row 4 (RS): With MC, 2ch, 1htr in each st across.
Work last 4 rows a further 3 times placing a locking stitch marker at each end of Row 3 on last rep.

Next Row: With MC, 2ch, 1htr in each st across.

Next Row (RS): With CC, 1ch, 1dc in FLO of each st.

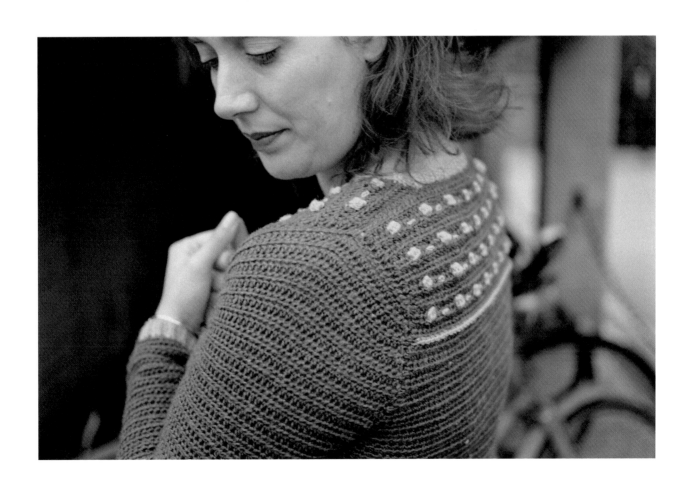

Fasten off and break CC. Without turning, start again at beginning of row and with MC, 2ch, 1htr in BLO of each st.

Next Row: With MC, 2ch, 1htr in each htr from previous row.

Work 0 (0, 4, 0, 2, 6, 7, 6, 5) rows straight in htr.

Shape armholes as follows:

Note: 2 sts increased by working 2htr in second and penultimate st.

Working in htr, inc 2 sts as set for the next 8 (10, 8, 14, 14, 12, 13, 16, 19) rows. 65 (76, 79, 91, 91, 94, 96, 102, 108) sts

Fasten off and break yarn.

Right Front (beginning at shoulder)

With RS facing, rejoin MC to other side of foundation ch for the Back (where the yarn tail is).

Set-up Row: 2ch, begin in same st as ch, work 14 (14, 14, 14, 14, 21, 21, 21, 21)htr in foundation ch for Back.

Work 20 rows of colourwork pattern as for Back and place marker at armhole edge as for Back.

Work 0 (0, 0, 0, 0, 6, 7, 6, 5) rows straight in htr.

Continue in htr throughout and shape armhole and neckline as follows:

Size M ONLY: Shape neck only, inc 1 st at neck edge for 4 rows. 18 sts.

ALL sizes again:

Shape armhole only by increasing at armhole edge for 3 (2, 0, 2, 4, 4, 5, 8, 11) rows. 17 (16, 18, 16, 18, 25, 26, 29, 32) sts

Shape armhole and neck edge by increasing at both edges for 1 (4, 4, 8, 8, 4, 4, 4, 4) rows. 19 (24, 26, 32, 34, 33, 34, 37, 40) sts

Increase 1 st at armhole edge and 2 sts at neck edge for 4 rows. 31 (36, 38, 44, 46, 45, 46, 49, 52) sts
Fasten off and break yarn.

Left Front (beginning at shoulder)

With RS facing, rejoin MC 14 (14, 14, 14, 14, 21, 21, 21, 21) st in from edge on foundation ch for Back. Work as for Right Front but do not fasten off or break yarn at end.

Join fronts and back to form body

Next Row (RS): 2ch, work 31 (36, 38, 44, 46, 45, 46, 49, 52)htr across Left Front, make 7 (5, 8, 8, 14, 22, 26, 32, 37)ch, work 65 (76, 79, 91, 91, 94, 96, 102, 108)htr across Back, make 7 (5, 8, 8, 14, 22, 26, 32, 37)ch, work 31 (36, 38, 44, 46, 45, 46, 49, 52)htr across Right Front.

Next Row (WS): 2ch, 1htr in each st and ch across. 141 (158, 171, 195, 211, 228, 240, 264, 286) sts
Work straight in htr until body measures 34cm / 13in from underarm ch.

Break yarn.

Hem

Using smaller hook, CC and with RS facing, join yarn at row end and make 7ch.

Row 1: Starting in third ch from hook, 5htr.
Row 2: Sl st in next 2 sts on Body, 5htr in BLO.
Row 3: 2ch, 5htr in BLO.
Rep Rows 2 and 3 until all sts on Body have been worked.

Sleeves (both alike)

Note: Do not count sl st as a stitch and do not work into the top of them.

With RS facing, join MC at the marker, starting in next row end, work 1htr in each row end to the row before the other marker. Sl st into marked row end, turn. 30 sts

Row 1: Work 1htr in each st across and 1htr into next free row end, sl st into next row end, turn. 1 st inc
Rep Row 1 until all row ends have been used. 46 (48, 50, 52, 54, 56, 58, 60, 62) sts

Next Row: 1htr in each st across, 4 (3, 4, 4, 7, 11, 13, 16, 19)dc in ch at undearm (this will work across half the chain), turn.

Next Row: 1ch, work 4 (3, 4, 4, 7, 11, 13, 16, 19)dc, work 1htr in each st and in each rem chain at underarm, sl st to join for working in the round. 53 (53, 58, 60, 68, 78, 84, 92, 99) sts.
Work in the round, turning at end of each round and dec 2 sts as follows: 1htr, 1htr2tog, htr to last 3 sts, 1htr2tog, 1htr every 8 (8, 7, 6, 4, 3, 3, 2, 2) rounds until 39 (39, 42, 42, 42, 42, 48, 48, 51) sts remain.

Work straight until sleeve measures 43cm / 17in from underarm.

Fasten off and break yarn.

Cuffs

Using smaller hook and CC, join yarn at round end, make 7ch.

Row 1: Starting in third ch from hook, 5htr.
Row 2: Sl st in next 2 sts on body, 5htr in BLO.
Row 3: 2ch, 5htr in BLO.

Rep Rows 2 and 3 until all sts on cuff have been worked.

Neck Edging

With RS facing, using smaller hook and CC, join yarn at neck edge, make 5ch.

Row 1: Starting in third ch from hook, 3htr.
Row 2: Sl st in next 2 rows ends of neck, 3htr in BLO.
Row 3: 2ch, 3htr in BLO.

Rep Rows 2 and 3 until all sts on neck have been worked. Note: When working across the back neck, slip stitch over three stitches and use your judgement when slip stitching around the curves to ensure a smooth band.

Button Bands

Left band:

With WS facing, using smaller hook and CC, join yarn on Left Front, make 7ch.

Row 1: Starting in third ch from hook, 5htr.
Row 2: Sl st in next 2 row ends on Front, 5htr in BLO.
Row 3: 2ch, 5htr in BLO.

Rep rows 2 and 3 until all rows of front and neck edging are worked.

Right band:

Work Right Front button band as Left and add six evenly spaced buttonholes as follows:

Row 2: Sl st in next 2 row ends on Front, 2htr in BLO, 1ch, miss 1htr, 2htr in BLO.

Row 3: 2ch, 2htr in BLO, 1htr in ch-sp, 2htr in BLO.

Finishing

Weave in ends and block lightly.

Using buttonholes as a guide for placement, sew on buttons.

Abbreviations

BLO	Back loop only
cn	Cable needle
ch	Chain
ch-sp	Chain space
CC	Contrast colour
dec	Decrease(d)
dc	Double crochet (US: Single crochet)
FLO	Front loop only
htr	Half treble crochet (US: Half double crochet)
htr2tog	Half treble 2 stitches together (US: Half double 2 stitches together)
inc	Increase(d)
k	Knit
kfb	Knit into the front then the back of one stitch
k2tog	Knit two stitches together
LH	Left hand
MC	Main colour
pm	Place marker
p	Purl
patt	Pattern
rep	Repeat
RS	Right side
sl	Slip
sm	Slip marker
ssk	Slip one knitwise, slip one purlwise, knit two slipped stiches together
st(s)	Stitch(es)
St st	Stocking stitch (US: Stockinette)
tbl	Through the back loop
tog	Together
tr	Treble crochet (US: Double crochet)
tr2tog	Treble crochet two stitches together (US: Double crochet two stitches together)
WS	Wrong side
yo	Yarn over
yrh	Yarn round hook

Note – stitches specific to certain patterns such as cables etc are with their pattern

On location

Bletchley Park, in Milton Keynes, Buckinghamshire, was the central site of the United Kingdom's Code and Cypher School (GC&CS). Known as the 'Code Breakers', this is where a team of cryptographic experts, supported by a team of administrative staff, cracked the Enigma and Lorenz cyphers. This gave them access to intelligence on enemy movements, which gave the Allies the upper hand in several decisive battles during World War II.

Geographically located 50 miles north-west of London, Bletchley was on the main Oxford to Cambridge railway line and close to the West Coast main line. This gave easy access for the academics that were to become code breakers, and the nearby telephone and telegraph exchange allowed high volume communication links needed for the operation.

Alan Turing and the team at Bletchley Park made several pioneering advances during their time there, which it is estimated shortened the war in Europe by two - four years.

Bletchley Park is now a heritage site and tourist attraction, open to the public. More information can be found at **www.bletchleypark.org.uk**

Steel

A simply stunning neutral. A beautiful, classic shade, Steel works equally well on its own or as a background to some of the other fabulous shades in this range. Featured in the Hut 8 and as the main colour for Bombe, Steel could also be used to make a striking Colossus, allowing the cables to shine.

Rust

Warm and vibrant. This vivid shade offers a rich, warm hue perfect as an accent colour but equally well suited to the wonderful garments in this collection. Featured in Tunny and Bombe.

Damson

Rich and sophisticated. This jewel toned shade has such incredible depth. Featured in Bombe, Colossus and Baudot, Damson really compliments the design details in these knits. It would also make an opulent Morse Code.

Harvest Gold

Sunshine in a skein. The shimmer of the silk and the glorious colour of this shade make it the perfect compliment to the richer shades in the range. Featured in Tunny, Bombe and Morse Code. It would make a fabulous Baudot, bringing a touch of sunshine to your every day wardrobe.

Night Sky

Elegant and refined. A sumptuous shade, perfect for showcasing the magnificent designs in this collection. Featured in Morse Code, Bombe and Tunny. This beautiful shade would also create a sophisticated Hut 8.

The Yarn

The flagship yarn in our mill dyed range, the luxurious Milburn 4ply, is a sumptuous blend of 85% Blue Faced Leicester and 15% silk. With the strength, lustre and durability of British Bluefaced Leicester complimented perfectly by the smooth sheen of silk, this yarn is versatile enough for everyday garments that add a touch of class, as well as precious, delicate, accent projects.

The yarn is specifically designed by us and receives extra combings at the mill, to ensure perfect blending. This creates a more luxurious feeling, drapey yarn that shimmers and glows, with rich depth of colour and added tones. With a fairly high twist, you get all the glamour of the silk, yet amplify the resilience of the Bluefaced Leicester, meaning your garments will wear well, yet continue to look as good as the day you finished them.

Available in seven shades, with neutrals as well as complimentary pairings to make the colours in your projects sing, Milburn 4ply is supplied in 50g skeins.

Victoria Magnus

Victoria Magnus is an independent hand dyer and knitwear designer, and the woman behind Eden Cottage Yarns. Based in Yorkshire, Victoria is inspired by nature and her surroundings, and hand dyes all her yarns in her home kitchen. Every aspect of the operation takes place here, from preparation to finishing and labeling of skeins, ready to grace your needles. Passionate about simplicity and wearability in her designs, Victoria loves to create garments and accessories that are versatile enough to use every day.

Stocked worldwide, Eden Cottage Yarns specialises in high quality natural fibres, dyed to a relaxing and understated palette, to allow the beauty to shine through in your projects.

Contact details

Yarns, pattern books and much more available on the **website**
http://www.edencottageyarns.co.uk

Digital patterns available from **Ravelry**
http://www.ravelry.com/patterns/sources/eden-cottage-yarns

Join in the chatter on the **Ravelry Group**
http://www.ravelry.com/groups/eden-cottage

Find us on **social media**
Twitter: @edencottage
Instagram: EdenCottageYarns
Facebook: https://www.facebook.com/pages/Eden-Cottage-Yarns/151573411577273

Email: edencottageyarns@gmail.com

Find **Joanne Scrace** online at www.notsogranny.com

Notes

Code Breaker

Lightning Source UK Ltd.
Milton Keynes UK
UKIC01n2314220115
244972UK00012B/97